The Wild World of Animals

Elephants

Trunks and Tusks

by Adele D. Richardson

Consultant:
Anne Warner
Director of Conservation and Education
The Oakland Zoo

Bridgestone Books
an imprint of Capstone Press
Mankato, Minnesota

Bridgestone Books are published by Capstone Press
151 Good Counsel Drive, P.O. Box 669, Mankato, Minnesota 56002
http://www.capstone-press.com

Library of Congress Cataloging-in-Publication Data
Richardson, Adele, 1966–
    Elephants: trunks and tusks/ by Adele D. Richardson.
    p. cm.—(The wild world of animals)
    Includes bibliographical references (p. 24) and index.
    ISBN 0-7368-0962-7
    1. Elephants—Juvenile literature. [1. Elephants.] I. Title. II. Series.
QL737.P98 R527 2002
599.67—dc21
                                                      00-012539

Summary: An introduction to elephants describing their physical characteristics, habitat,
    young, food, predators, and relationship to people.

Editorial Credits
Erika Mikkelson, editor; Karen Risch, product planning editor; Linda Clavel, cover designer
    and illustrator; Heidi Schoof, photo researcher

Photo Credits
Craig Brandt, 4
Index Stock Imagery, cover
PhotoDisc, Inc., 1
Robin Brandt, 16
Russel Kriete/Root Resources, 8
Stan Osdiniski/Root Resources, 6
Tom & Pat Leeson, 10, 12, 18, 20
Visuals Unlimited/Hal Beral, 14

1 2 3 4 5 6 07 06 05 04 03 02

Table of Contents

African elephant

ear

tusks

tail

trunk

legs

Elephants

Elephants have four huge legs and four round feet. Elephants have trunks. Most elephants have ivory tusks. Two kinds of elephants live in the world. Asian elephants have smaller ears and bodies than African elephants. Female Asian elephants do not have tusks.

tusks
long, curved teeth

Asian elephants

FUN FACTS

Asian elephants have ears that are three times smaller than African elephants' ears.

Elephants Are Mammals

Elephants are mammals. Mammals are warm-blooded animals with a backbone. Female mammals feed milk to their young. Elephants are the largest mammals that live on land.

warm-blooded
having a body temperature that stays the same

African elephants

FUN FACTS

African elephants can grow to be 13 feet (4 meters) tall and weigh 14,000 pounds (6,300 kilograms). Male elephants are larger than female elephants.

An Elephant's Habitat

Elephants live in Africa and Asia. Asian elephants' habitat is forests. African elephants roam large open grasslands called savannas. Other African elephants live in forests.

habitat
the place where
an animal lives

An Elephant's Trunk

Elephants can pick up many objects with their trunks. Elephants use their trunks to suck up water or mud. They spray the water into their mouths. Elephants spray mud on their bodies for protection from insects and the hot sun.

African elephant

What Do Elephants Eat?

Elephants are herbivores. They eat grass, fruit, tree bark, and plants. They sometimes knock down trees to reach the highest leaves. Elephants use their tusks to tear bark from trees. They also use their tusks to dig up plant roots.

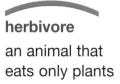

herbivore
an animal that eats only plants

African elephants

Mating and Birth

Female elephants and their young live in herds. Male elephants find female elephants when it is time to mate. Female elephants give birth about 22 months later. One young elephant usually is born at a time.

mate
to join together
to produce young

African elephant calf

Elephant Calves

Young elephants are calves. Newborn calves weigh about 250 pounds (110 kilograms) and stand 3 feet (1 meter) tall. Female calves stay near their mothers for their whole lives. Male calves leave their mothers when they are 11 to 18 years old.

Predators

Elephants protect themselves from predators. Lions, wild dogs, and hyenas sometimes attack elephant calves. Adult elephants make a circle around the calves to protect them. Elephants stick out their ears to look bigger. They charge at a predator if it does not leave.

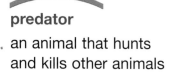

predator
an animal that hunts
and kills other animals

Asian elephant and calf

Elephants and People

Elephants have helped people for many years. Some elephants are trained to lift and carry objects for people. Some people have harmed elephants. Many elephants have been killed for their ivory tusks. Today, it is illegal to kill elephants.

Hands On: Hearing Low Sounds

Elephants make many sounds. People cannot hear some of the sounds because they are too low. You can make and hear a low sound by doing this activity.

What You Need

An 18-inch (46-centimeter) long piece of string
Rubber band
Metal spoon

What You Do

1. Tie the string to the rubber band.
2. Wrap the rubber band around the handle of the spoon until it is tight.
3. Wrap the other end of the string gently around one finger. Now cover each of your ears with one hand. Hang on to the string with one hand.
4. Move your body so the spoon gently taps on a table or a wall.

You will hear the sound of the spoon hitting the table or wall. You also will hear the sound of the spoon vibrating. The vibration travels up the string and your finger into your ear. The vibrations then are turned into sound. Elephants can make and hear even lower sounds than the spoon made.

Words to Know

herd (HURD)—a large group of animals; female elephants and their calves live together in herds.

mammal (MAM-uhl)—a warm-blooded animal that has a backbone; female mammals feed milk to their young.

mate (MATE)—to join together to produce young; male and female elephants mate to produce elephant calves.

predator (PRED-uh-tur)—an animal that hunts and eats other animals

warm-blooded (warm-BLUHD-id)—having a body temperature that stays the same

Read More

Butterfield, Moira. *Big, Rough, and Wrinkly.* What Am I? Austin, Texas: Raintree Steck-Vaughn, 1997.

Holmes, Kevin J. *Elephants.* Animals. Mankato, Minn.: Bridgestone Books, 2000.

Schwabacher, Martin. *Elephants.* New York: Marshall Cavendish, 2000.

Internet Sites

The African Elephant
http://worldkids.net/critters/mammals/elephant.htm
Asian Elephant
http://www.sazoo-aq.org/indeleph.html
Elephant
http://www.EnchantedLearning.com/subjects/mammals/elephant/Elephantcoloring.shtml

Index